Magnetic Field Application

Bringing Harmony and Balance to Your Body

By R. Allen Walls

INNER SEARCH FOUNDATION, INC.
MCLEAN, VIRGINIA

We must act as though we were the masters of our destiny, as though all things were bound to obey us; and yet in our soul resides the true knowing to give over in noble submission to the mighty spiritual forces we will inevitably encounter.

Maurice Maeterlinck
Wisdom & Destiny—1903

A Few Words from the Author

The purpose of this handbook is to help you learn how to improve and maintain your health by using Magnetic Field Application to relieve stress and physical discomfort and to balance the overall energy field of your body.

In my work as a therapist I use a total approach to wellness to help my clients achieve a positive spiritual, mental and physical condition.

The body is affected by all of the various conditions it is exposed to daily. Keeping the physical body in harmony and in proper balance is crucial. How well your body functions is dependent upon a complex interaction among the food you eat, everything you ingest or inhale (which could include addictive drugs, smoke, and harmful amounts of other substances), negative or positive environmental conditions, the amount of exercise you get, the amount of stress in your life, the atmosphere of love within and around you, and your connectedness with the positive forces in the universe.

Using Magnetic Field Application is a step toward taking command of your well-being and can lead you to an increased awareness of the value and importance of self care. It opens a new way for self examination. Explore all the areas of your body and feel how your energy field reacts to the use of Magnetic Field Application. The effect may be dramatic or may occur subtly over a period of time. Whichever effect occurs, you will be improving your health.

Happy days, a full and pleasurable life, can be yours whenever you are ready to put your spiritual, physical and mental health at the top of your list.

Take responsibility for your total well-being. Start NOW!

R. Allen Walls

About the Author

R. Allen Walls is a behavioral and core-energetic therapist. He is President of Inner Search Foundation, Inc., an educational and spiritual-development, non-profit, tax-exempt organization. Mr. Walls is the author of the book, *Life Plan, Finding Your Real Self, The Journey Through Life.* For more than fifteen years as a therapist, he has realized the value of practicing a comprehensive approach to wellness along with developing a positive spiritual consciousness. He helps his clients connect with their higher purpose and overall sense of well being.

Dedication and Acknowledgments

This book is for my wife, Mari, who has helped me in every way with her loving support and encouragement, and for my children, Justin and Farrah, who have used Magnetic Field Application and support my healing work.

My thanks and appreciation to the following persons who have contributed immeasurably to the production of the book: Luella Murri for her dedication in editing the book with careful attention to the many details; Mary Anne Diaz, who made the graphics and typeset so completely readable and understandable; and Al Crook for his original idea and for allowing this publication to become a reality.

Published by:

Inner Search Foundation, Inc.
P.O. Box 10382
McLean, VA 22102-1502

Library of Congress Cataloging-in-Publication Data
Walls, R. Allen 1941
Magnetic Field Application Handbook
1. Magnetism and Energy - Therapeutic Use
Bibliography
ISBN - 0-9621790-4-3

Other Books By The Author
Life Plan: Finding Your Real Self
(ISBN #0-9-621790-1-9)

Table of Contents

Introduction

Section 1 —Magnetic Field Application — Acupressure Method

Section 2 — Magnetic Field Application
— Short and Long- Term Usages

Table of Contents (cont.)

Section 3 — Articles and Excerpts concerning Magnetic Field Therapy

Human beings evolved and live within the earth's magnetic field, which is essential to the life of every living cell. However, scientific measurements show that the strength of the magnetic field has decreased over the centuries. Animals die if shielded from the earth's magnetic force. Many of us spend a large part of our time in buildings which block the magnetic field. Furthermore, the alternating current (AC) coming from electrical and electronic appliances and equipment in home and workplace interferes with the earth's natural magnetic field and is harmful to the cells.

Magnetic Field Application products have now been designed especially to provide the magnetism needed for total body wellness, as well as to subtly stimulate the body's own healing mechanism in the case of stress and specific physical problems. The recommended products are those with a strength of fewer than 1,000 gauss, since magnets with a higher strength should be used only under professional supervision. The magnets are permanent and can be used indefinitely without losing their strength.

This Magnetic Field Application handbook has been prepared to help people who seek overall well-being, as well as those who suffer from discomfort and specific physical problems.

The handbook describes two different ways to use specially designed flexible magnetic application pads. The triangular arrangement of north and south poles makes these pads more effective than ordinary magnets.

Section One describes the Acupressure Method, in which magnetic application pads are held briefly on specific points along the acupressure meridians (energy channels) to increase and balance the flow of energy through the body. The placement of the magnets corresponds with acupuncture application.

Section Two describes the Short- and Long-Term Usages of magnetic application pads to problem areas of the body to increase energy flow and circulation and to stimulate the body's draining system, thus bringing more oxygen and nutrients to the cells and tissues and speeding the elimination of toxic wastes. Both methods can be understood easily and used effectively by anyone, either professional or lay person, with the same results as those obtained by an experienced practitioner.

Section Two describes also the use and benefits of other Magnetic Field Application products for Total Body Wellness.

Numerous studies have established the positive effect of Magnetic Field Application on the human body. See the references listed at the end of this handbook. The body heals itself over time, as many "permanent" ailments begin to correct themselves.

Biomagnetic Research Continues

Around the world, research on the therapeutic potential of magnetism is continuing, and the publication, *Journal of Bioelectricity*, is devoted to the field. Among the places where this leading edge technology is being studied are Loma Linda University in San Diego; New York University; the Massachusetts Institute of Technology; the Institute for Magnetotherapy in Madras, India; the University of Leeds in England; the University of Colorado; the University of South Carolina; the University of California in San Francisco; Columbia University in New York; Florida State University; and scores of other laboratories and institutions in Japan, Germany, Sweden and other nations.

[One] scientist whose comprehensive studies of magnetic fields and healing have been widely published is Physicist/Psychologist Dr. Buryl Payne, inventor of the first biofeedback instruments and former professor at Boston University and Goddard College. His recent books, *The Body Magnetic* and *Getting Started in Magnetic Healing* have served as authoritative handbooks for professionals and lay people alike.

According to Dr. Payne, sensitive research instruments have allowed scientists to document some of the ways magnetic fields affect living organisms. He cites specific factors now known to be involved in magnetic healing. Among them are:

• Improved ennergy circulation;

• Changes in migration of calcium ions which can either bring calcium ions to heal a broken bone in half the usual time, or can help move calcium away from joint discomfort;

• The pH balance (acid/alkaline) of various body fluids (often out of balance in conjunction with illness or abnorrnal conditions) can apparently be altered by magnetic fields;

• Hormone production from the endocrine glands can be either increased or decreased by magnetic stimulation;

• Altering of enzyme activity and other bio-chemical processes.

As an example of specific effects created when a magnetic field is applied to the body, below are typical changes that have been documented:

• Electricity is generated in blood vessels;

• Ionized particles increase in the blood;

• Autonomic nerves are excited;

• Circulation is improved.

To better understand the implications of providing the body with an adequate magnetic environment, it is irnportant to understand the basic movement of certain body fluids and their role in health and disease.

In a somewhat simplified explanation, as the heart pumps approx-imately 80 times per minute, blood in the arteries forces nutrient-laden liquid through pores in the capillaries into the cell area to nourish the cells. (This liquid is called plasma while it is in the bloodstream and is re-named "lymph" once it leaves the bloodstream.)

The blood proteins in the vessels have a high affinity for water, and aid in pulling liquid back into the blood vessels. Through the venous system, the "used" blood is returned to the heart and lungs for purification and re-charging.

Because each individual cell, and the body as a whole, is an electrical generator, the cells must have oxygen to convert glucose into energy, and the balance of potassium/sodium within each cell must remain correct to keep the generators going.

The blood plasma contains numerous cells and protein molecules suspended in it. Under ordinary conditions, the normal blood pressure causes some of the blood proteins to continually seep through the tiny capillary pores into the spaces around the cells. There is not enough pressure in the cells to push these proteins back through the pores, so they must be continually removed and returned to the blood stream via the lymphatic system.

Discomfort and illness begin when conditions cause the capillary pores to dilate and allow the escape of significant quantities of blood proteins into the cellular area. This crowding of the proteins attracts fluid (inflammation), causes pain, and deprives some of the cells in the area of proper oxygen and nutrients, resulting in poor cellular functioning. These malfunctioning cells, if not carried away and disposed of by the lymphatic system, begin to destroy healthy cells and may keep proliferating into cancer or re-enter the bloodstream and cause leukemia.

If the lymphatic system completely fails to function and these blood proteins become trapped throughout the body, death can occur within hours.

According to Dr. C. Samuel West, chemist and internationally recognized lymphologist, trapped blood proteins are the one common denominator present in all pain and disease....

In citing circumstances which can cause trapped blood proteins, Dr. West lists the following: shallow breathing, improper exercise, shock, stress, anger, fear, tea, coffee, liquor, tobacco, drugs, salt, sugar, fat, high-cholesterol food, too much meat and others.

Many years of research and clinical application have shown that the simple introduction of a magnetic field can provide stimulation and enhancement of the lymphatic system, as well as every cell within the body. The magnetic field does not heal; it merely aids the cells in creating an optimum environment in which the body can begin to heal itself. Between the circulatory, lymphatic and neurological effects, outstanding advances in health can be obtained.

Many biomagnetic practitioners are now offering education, treatment, and magnetic devices to those seeking alternative health care. Among the most viable of these options is a magnetic sleep system developed in Japan. Users are able to sleep nightly within a cocoon of balanced magnetic energy to revitalize their bodies, with the system providing ongoing effectiveness levels.

The Healing Crisis

A healing crisis is in effect when the body is in the process of elimination. Reactions may be mild or they may be severe. One should expect this and work toward it. The body's inherent desire is perfect health. We have the ability to earn our way back to that state. The body must go through an elimination process to achieve good health. There will be ups and downs. One does not go immediately into good health. This elimination process we call the "healing process."

A healing crisis results when all body systems work in concert to eliminate waste products and set the stage for regeneration. Old tissues are replaced with new. A disease crisis, on the other hand, is not a natural one and works against the body's natural processes. Symptoms during a healing crisis may be identical to the disease, but there is an important difference—elimination. A cleansing, purifying process is underway and stored wastes are in a free-flowing state. Sometimes pain during the healing crisis is of greater intensity than when the chronic disease is building up. This may explain why there may be a brief flare-up in one's condition.

The crisis will usually bring about past conditions in whatever order the body is capable of handling them at the time. People often forget the disease or injuries they have had in the past, but are usually reminded during crisis. Reactions could include skin eruptions, nausea, headache, sleepiness, unusual fatigue, diarrhea, head or chest cold, ear infections, boils, or any other way the body uses to loosen and eliminate toxins. The crisis usually lasts three days, but if the energy of the patient is low it may last for a week or more. The body needs juices, and especially water, to help carry off the toxins. This is a time for rest—mental as well as physical rest.

One crisis is not always enough for a complete cure. The person in a chronic state, who has gone through many disease processes in life, must go through these processes again. Often the crisis will come after one feels his very best, setting the stage for the action. Most people feel an energy boost the first few days. Then toxins are dumped into the blood stream for elimination. Go as slowly as your body needs to so that your elimination is gradual and comfortable.

With a more serious condition there may be many small crises to go through before the final one is possible. Everything must be considered and given its proper place in the build-up to a healing crisis. One should expect it and work towards it.

Section 1

Magnetic Field Application

Acupressure Method

In the Acupressure Method of Magnetic Field Application two magnetic application pads are held briefly on specific points along the acupressure meridians (energy channels) to increase and balance the flow of energy through the body. The magnetic application pad to be used is the small pad, which is about the size of a silver dollar and has a strength of 700 gauss, or the maxi, which is 3 1/2" in diameter and has a strength of 650 gauss.

The procedures described in this section can be performed person-to-person or can be self-administered. Each of the recommended procedures is specifically related to certain ailments. The first stage, identified as "Greeting," is essential to the overall process. Do the Greeting first, followed by the procedure for "Metabolism," then go on to the specific procedure to treat the area or condition requiring attention.

Once a procedure has been completed and the corrective process is started, it is advisable to let the body have time to "cycle" before another treatment is administered. A minimum of one or two hours is adequate.

Cautions and Proper Usage

You may wish to discuss this application with your doctor. Certainly, a physician should be consulted concerning any serious problem. No medical claims are made for Magnetic Field Application nor are there any inferences that it is a substitute for conventional medical techniques. Magnetic Field Application is used to increase energy flow, relax tense muscles, relieve musculo-skeletal discomfort, and accelerate the body's own healing process.

Magnets work differently on each individual. There is no guarantee expressed or implied that magnets will relieve your particular tension, relieve your particular discomfort, or accelerate the healing process for your particular injury. They work with varying results in varying time frames for each individual. You will need to experiment with the use, placement, and effect of the magnets on your problem area. The magnets may not be effective for you in all of the cited situations.

Cautions and Proper Usage (cont.)

Under no condition should Magnetic Field Application be used by persons wearing cardiac pace-makers or defibrillators, since they are electromagnetically programmed. Wait 24 to 48 hours after suffering a sprain, hematoma, or wound before applying magnetic application pads. Adherence to the acronym RICE (R=Rest, I=Ice, C=Compression, E=Elevation) is best during this period to reduce swelling. It is recommended also that Magnetic Field Application not be used by women in the first trimester of pregnancy.

Do not allow credit cards, cassette tapes, video tapes, watches or other electronic equipment to come in contact with any magnetic product.

Do not stack one magnet on top of another, since the higher strength may increase the discomfort.

The magnetic application pads can be applied over light clothing or directly on the skin. Place the cloth side toward the body. Be sure the skin where you will be placing the magnets is clean. The cloth pads on the magnets will absorb ointments, rubs, Vaseline, or any other surface medication. (Note: Removal of the cloth pad will not harm the magnet. However, should yours wear out or become detached, adhesive-backed moleskin works very well as a replacement.)

Problem Areas or Conditions and Applicable Procedures

The following list shows the various problem areas or conditions which can be treated, together with the applicable procedures to use:

Problem Area or Condition	Use Procedures For:	Page
Facial Discomfort	infection	35
Pre-senile dementia	metabolism; head; neck	23, 28, 32
Heart problems	upper back; heart; lungs	25, 29, 31
Anxiety	skin irritation	33
Stomach	abdomen (before an attack)	24
Arm problems	neck; shoulder; local	32, 28
Joint problems	metabolism; local	23, 30
Breathing problems	lungs; skin irritation	31, 33
Fluid movement	upper back; heart	25, 29
Injury	metabolism; local	23, 30
Chest congestion	metabolism; cold & flu; lungs	23, 30, 31
Feet swelling	metabolism; lower back; local	23, 25, 30
Cell disorders	metabolism; upper back; local	23, 25, 30
Cholesterol	metabolism	23
Circulation	heart	30
Colds and flu	upper back; cold & flu; sinus	25, 30, 35
Difficult evacuation	abdomen; lower back	24, 25
Digesting difficulty	metabolism; local	23, 30
Sacs with fluid matter	metabolism; upper back; local	23, 25, 30
Abnormal sugar processing	metabolism; upper back	23, 25
Diverticulitis	abdomen; lower back	23, 25
Abnormal chromosome	head; neck; local	28, 32, 30
Abnormal lung distention	upper back along spine; lungs	25, 31
Nervous system disorders	head	28

Note: "Local" means where the pain is.

Problem Area or Condition	Use Procedures For:	Page
Reproduction problems	abdomen; lower back (on men, work tailbone)	23, 25
Fingers (numb or tingle)	neck; shoulder; local	32, 34, 30
Foot problems	lower back; local	25, 28
Increased eye pressure	metabolism; eyes	23, 27
Uric acid excess	metabolism; local	23, 30
Head discomfort	head; neck	28, 32
Heart problems	heart	29
Anal Piles	abdomen; lower back (tailbone)	24, 25
Tissue protrusion	abdomen; lower back	24, 25
Hiatal hernia	solar plexus	36
Hormone troubles	abdomen; lower back	24, 25
Low glucose levels	metabolism	23
Digesting difficulties	solar plexus	36
Infection	cold & flu	30
Flu	cold & flu	30
Knee and leg problems	lower back; local	25, 30
Excessive cell production	metabolism; upper back; solar plexus	23, 25, 36
Lupus	metabolism; upper back; cold & flu; local	23, 25, 30,
Feminine aging	abdomen; lower back	24, 25
Menstrual discomfort	abdomen	25
Severe head discomfort	head; neck	28, 32
Brain & spinal problems	metabolism; whole back; head; neck	23, 25, 28, 32
Nervous stomach	skin irritation; solar plexus	27, 30
Bone disease	back	25
Nerve discomfort	head; neck (repeatedly)	25, 32
Lower body injury	back	25

Problem Area or Condition	Use Procedures For:	Page
Lung	metabolism; upper back; cold & flu; lungs	23, 25, 30, 31
Pregnancy (to ease delivery)	abdomen; lower back	24, 25
Skin disease	skin irritation	33
Hip/thigh pain	lower back	25
Back curving	metabolism; entire back	23, 25
Skin virus	skin irritation	33
Shoulder	shoulder	34
Sinus	facial discomfort	35
Stomach nerves	solar plexus	36
Stress	skin irritation	35
Stroke	upper back; head; heart; neck	25, 28, 29, 32
Swelling proturbance	metabolism; upper back; local	23, 25, 28
Open sores	skin irritation; solar plexus	27, 30
Liquid waste elimination	abdomen; lower back	24, 25
Swollen veins	metabolism; lower back; heart; local	23, 24, 25, 28
Small skin protrusions	metabolism; local	23, 28

To begin, do the "Greeting," then the "Metabolism," and then proceed to the area requiring attention. Problems of a serious nature can be addressed every hour or two. For maintenance and continued relief, apply as needed.

Greeting

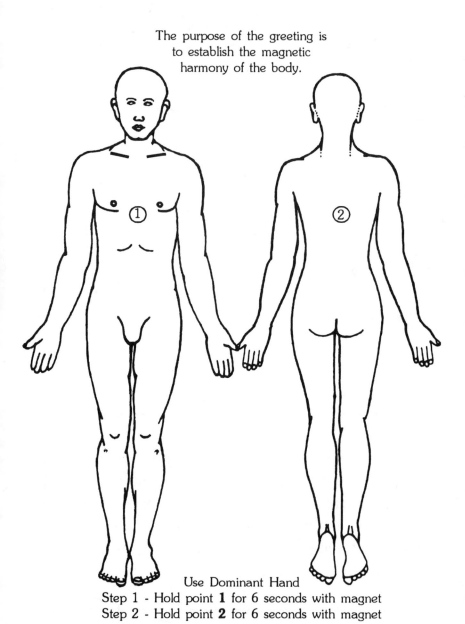

The purpose of the greeting is to establish the magnetic harmony of the body.

Use Dominant Hand
Step 1 - Hold point **1** for 6 seconds with magnet
Step 2 - Hold point **2** for 6 seconds with magnet

Step 1 - Use magnets to work points **1** through **3**, for 6 seconds each. Repeat 3 times.

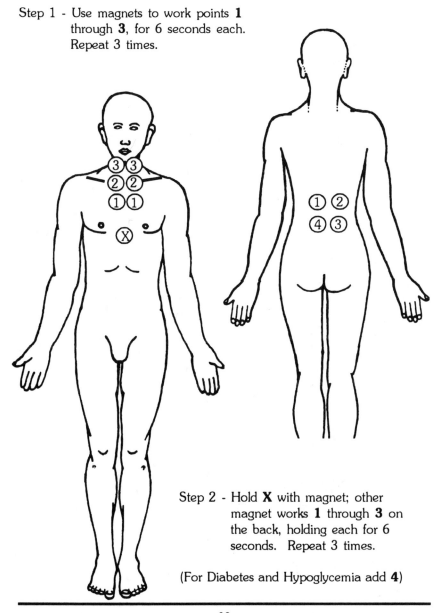

Step 2 - Hold **X** with magnet; other magnet works **1** through **3** on the back, holding each for 6 seconds. Repeat 3 times.

(For Diabetes and Hypoglycemia add **4**)

Step 1 - Hold **X** with magnet; other magnet works **1** through **5**, for 6 seconds each.

Step 2 - Hold **T** point on "Back" chart at sacrum "triangle;" with other magnet work **1** through **5** and **X** for 6 seconds each.

Step 3 - With two magnets work **1** & **X**; **2** & **3**; **4** & **5**, for 6 seconds each.

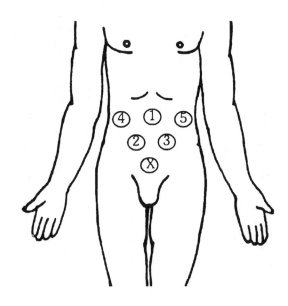

Step 1 - Hold **X** with magnet on coccyx (tailbone), hold 2 magnets at base of skull at point **1** for 6 seconds.*

Step 2 - Continuing to hold at point **X**, the other magnet is held at point **2** at center of base of skull for 6 seconds.

Step 3 - Hold **T** with a magnet; other magnet works points **3** through **9**, for 6 seconds each.

Step 4 - With 2 magnets work points **10** - **17** for 6 seconds each, (approximately every other vertebra).

Step 5 - When magnets are at point **17** on both sides of the spine, draw them smoothly and slowly in a single sweep down to points **10**, curving them gently outward and lifting off.

*Only place in handbook where 3 magnets are required. Step can be completed by holding on point **1** on right side for 6 seconds, and moving to point **1** on left side for 6 seconds.

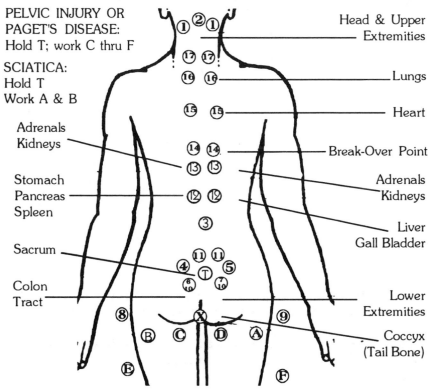

PELVIC INJURY OR
PAGET'S DISEASE:
Hold T; work C thru F

SCIATICA:
Hold T
Work A & B

Adrenals
Kidneys

Stomach
Pancreas
Spleen

Sacrum

Colon
Tract

Head & Upper
Extremities

Lungs

Heart

Break-Over Point

Adrenals
Kidneys

Liver
Gall Bladder

Lower
Extremities

Coccyx
(Tail Bone)

Note: 8 & 9 are on sides of hips. E & F are on sides of thighs.

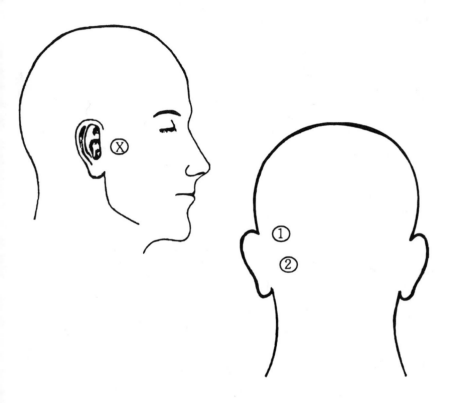

Step 1 - Hold **X** with magnet; other magnet works **1** and **2** on same side for 6 seconds then reverse sides for 6 seconds.

Step 2 - Work **X** on both sides of head; then **1** on both sides; then **2** on both sides, for 6 seconds each.

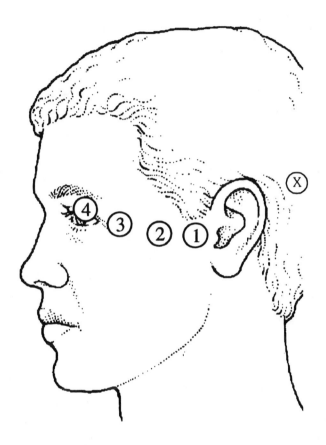

Step 1 - Hold **X** with magnet (first dent above rise); other magnet
works **1** through **4** on the same side for 6 seconds.

Step 2 - Reverse sides and repeat this set.

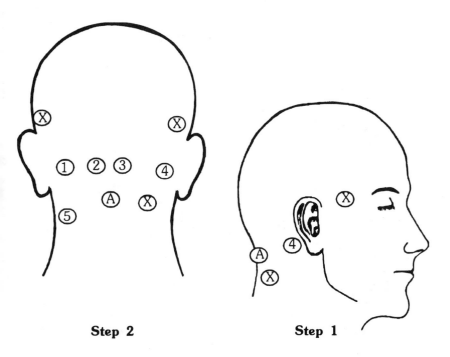

Step 2   **Step 1**

Step 1 - With finger on **X** beside the eye, hold magnet on other **X** with thumb; work **A** for 6 seconds.

Step 2 - Place one finger from each hand on two top **X**'s. Hold magnet on lower **X** with thumb while other magnet works opposite side **1** through **5** for 6 seconds each. Keep fingers on top **X**'s. Then, holding magnet on point **5** with thumb, use that as hold **X** while working other side **1** through **5** for 6 seconds each.

Step 3 - With two magnets work the left and right sides at the same time, points **1** - **5**, for 6 seconds each.

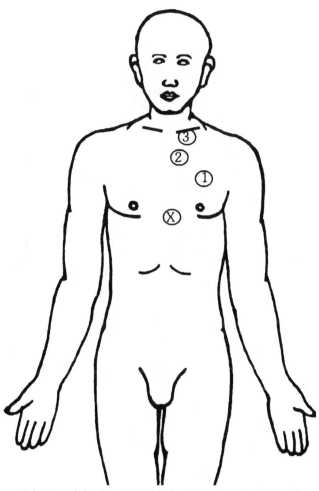

For major well-being of the heart, hold **X** with magnet, while other magnet works points **1** and **2** for 6 seconds each.   Repeat 3 times.
For circulation, veins, and blood pressure, hold **X** with magnet, while other magnet works **3**. Hold for 6 seconds. Repeat 3 times.

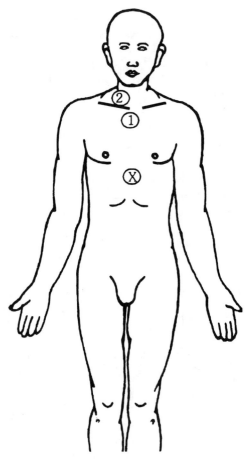

Infection & flu:
Hold **X** with magnet; with other magnet work **1** for 6 seconds.

Breathing Discomfort:
Hold **X** with magnet; with other magnet work **2** for 6 seconds. Repeat 3 times.

Oxygen Control Gland.

Step 1 - Hold **X** with magnet; other
magnet works **1** through **6**,
for 6 seconds each.

Step 2 - Use magnets at **1** and **4** ;
2 and **5**; **3** and **6**, for 6
seconds each.

Repeat each step 3 times, holding each
point for 6 seconds.

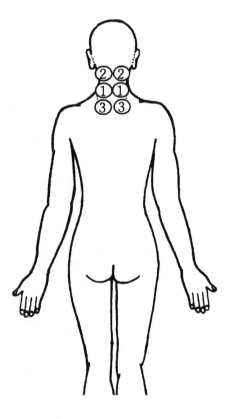

With two magnets work **1** through **3** for 6 seconds each. Repeat 3 times.

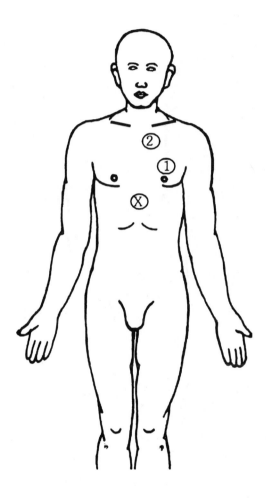

Hold **X** with magnet; other magnet works **1** and **2** for 6 seconds each. Repeat 3 times.

Shoulder

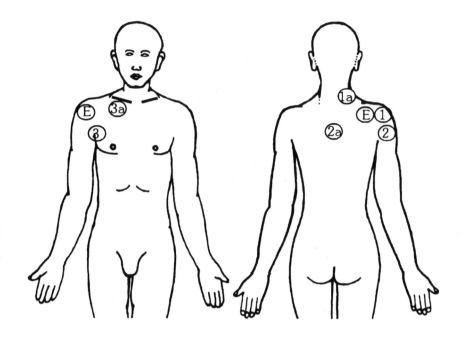

Step 1 - Hold magnet at **1**; use other magnet to sweep from 1 up line **1a** and down to **E**.

Step 2 - Hold magnet at **2**; use other magnet to sweep from 2 across line **2a** and up to **E**.

Step 3 - Hold magnet at **3**; use other magnet to sweep from 3 up line **3a** and across to **E**.

1 is the tip of the shoulder.
2 is indentation below back shoulder.
3 is indentation below front shoulder.

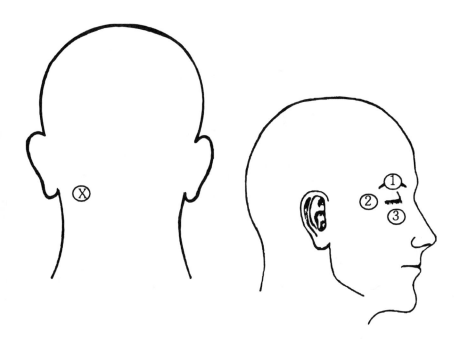

Step 1 - Hold **X** with magnet on left side; other magnet works **1**, **2**, and **3** on right side for 6 seconds each.

Step 2 - Hold **X** with magnet on right side; other magnet works **1**, **2** and **3** on left side. Hold each work point for 6 seconds.

Step 3 - Hold both **X** points with magnets for 6 seconds. Hold both **1** points with magnets for 6 seconds. Hold both **2** points with magnets for 6 seconds. Hold both **3** points with magnets for 6 seconds.

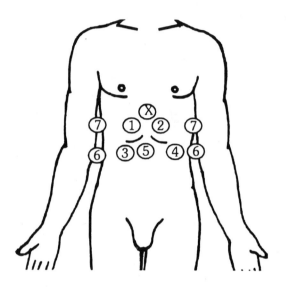

Step 1 - Hold **X** with magnet; other magnet works **1** through **7** for
6 seconds each.

Step 2 - Hold magnet just below ribs, while other
magnet works **1** through **7** and **X** for 6 seconds each.

Step 3 - With two magnets work **1** & **2**; **3** & **4**; **X** & **5**,
6's & **7**'s for 6 seconds each.

Note: **6** & **7** are on sides of torso.

Section 2

Magnetic Field Application

Short- and Long-Term

Usages

ISF

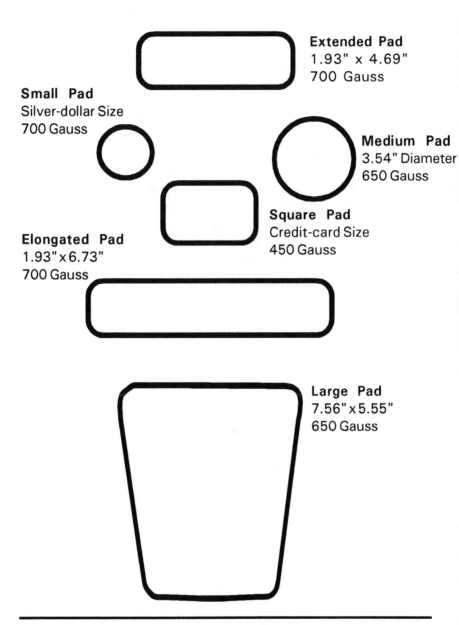

Extended Pad
1.93" x 4.69"
700 Gauss

Small Pad
Silver-dollar Size
700 Gauss

Medium Pad
3.54" Diameter
650 Gauss

Square Pad
Credit-card Size
450 Gauss

Elongated Pad
1.93" x 6.73"
700 Gauss

Large Pad
7.56" x 5.55"
650 Gauss

Use of Flexible Magnetic Application Pads

Flexible magnetic application pads can also be used very effectively without reference to the points along the acupressure meridians. However, in this case the pads must be left in place for a longer period of time. The pads are placed over the area of discomfort or at the point of origin of the pain.

The Extended, Small, Medium, Square, Elongated and Large Pads are designed to be used any time and any place to relieve muscular aches and pains and to relieve tension in the body. These patented pads, of positive and negative alternating polarity, bring relief to the affected area. They also stimulate the system. The body's own healing processes are accelerated by the increased activation of the immune system with the simultaneous removal of toxic waste products that result from injured tissue.

The use of the magnetic application pads is simple; just follow the suggestions to ensure proper results. The flexibility of the pads allows them to fit into everyone's life-style with the greatest of comfort. They can be cut to shape without losing their magnetic properties.

Cautions and Proper Usage

You may wish to discuss this application with your doctor. Certainly, a physician should be consulted concerning any serious problem. No medical claims are made for Magnetic Field Application nor are there any inferences that it is a substitute for conventional medical techniques. Magnetic Field Application is used to increase energy flow, relax tense muscles, relieve musculo-skeletal discomfort, and accelerate the body's own healing process by increasing blood flow and lymphatic circulation in the area under the influence of the magnet.

Magnets work differently on each individual. There is no guarantee expressed or implied that magnets will relieve your particular tension, relieve your particular pain, or accelerate the healing process for your particular injury. They work with varying results in varying time frames for each individual. You will need to experiment with the use, placement, and effect of the magnets on your problem area. The magnets may not be effective for you in all of the cited situations.

Under no condition should Magnetic Field Application be used by persons wearing cardiac pace-makers or defibrillators, since they are electromagnetically programmed. Wait 24 to 48 hours after suffering a sprain, hematoma, or wound before applying magnetic application pads. Adherence to the acronym RICE (R=Rest, I=Ice, C=Compression, E=Elevation) is best during this period to reduce swelling. It is recommended also that Magnetic Field Application not be used by women in the first trimester of pregnancy.

Do not stack one magnet on top of another, since the higher strength may increase the discomfort.

Do not place credit cards, cassette tapes, video tapes, watches or other electronic equipment on any magnetic products.

The magnetic application pads can be applied over light clothing or directly on the skin. Place the cloth side toward the body. Be sure the skin where you will be placing the magnets is clean. The cloth pads on the magnets will absorb ointments, rubs, Vaseline, or any other surface medication. (Note: Removal of the cloth pad will not harm the magnet. However, should yours wear out or become detached, adhesive-backed moleskin works very well as a replacement.)*

To hold the magnetic application pads in place use a knitted wristband or headband, elastic bandage (never neoprene), or paper tape for sensitive skin. Surgical tape is best (e.g., 3M Micropore tape, Curity's Tenderskin, or Dermicel by Johnson & Johnson). Avoid adhesive or Scotch tape, as these may remove the gold

*Can be ordered through Breakthrough Media, Inc.

Cautions and Proper Usage (cont.)

plating from the surface of the magnetic application pads.

A strip of male Velcro stuck to the back of a pad will hold the pad firmly in place inside a bandage or knitted band. If you will wish to remove the Velcro later, wrap the pad in plastic before applying the Velcro.

If possible, wear the pads 24 hours a day, removing them only when bathing. Water will not hurt the pads; in fact, they can be washed, but it is inadvisable to leave a wet pad next to the skin.

Suggestions for Short- and Long-Term Usages of Magnetic Field Application

Ankle

Square or Medium Pad

For fresh sprains, ice is used for the first 24 to 48 hours. Use a pad with male Velcro inside an Ace or similar ankle support. Continue to use for two days after discomfort is gone.

Breathing Discomfort

Medium Pad

Wear a Medium Pad the chest. Women can tuck one into their bra. A strip or two of male Velcro on the back of the pad will make it cling to a man's undershirt. Or place the pad inside a replacement pocket and fasten the flap over a chain or cord worn around the neck.

Extended, Small, Meduim, Square, Elongated or Large Pad

On the high back, the discomfort is nearly always a few inches from the spine to the right, to the left or both. In all cases, you will be able to find that area which is the most tender. Any of the pads mentioned can be used depending upon the size of the affected area. Always use one pad on each side of the high back, even if the discomfort is only on one side. If you treat only one side, the other side will compensate and a problem will be created where none previously existed. Affix the pads with flexible tape. Or stick male Velcro to the back of the pads and position them inside an undershirt or T-shirt.

For the lower back, the pads are taped over the areas of most discomfort, again on both sides. In addition, a pad can be taped to the center of the low back right over the spine. Men should take their wallets or any other items out of the rear pockets as these put pressure on the sciatic nerve, which makes the condition worse. Women can find the areas in the low back easily by looking for the slight depressions at the base of the back and above the buttocks. Place a magnetic application pad in each of those depressions with flexible tape.

A Large Pad may be used in place of any of the other pads. It covers a larger area and has Velcro strips attached to its rear surface so you can place it inside clothing and it won't shift around. It is especially useful for low-back pain. Care should be taken when going to the bathroom that you don't forget it is there and let if fall into the water. Since the Velcro can tear knitted underwear and pantyhose, you may wish to wear the Large Pad between your underwear and your outer clothing rather than next to the skin.

Bags Under The Eyes

Small Pad

This procedure may be used to temporarily reduce or eliminate bags under the eyes. This can be done every morning for as little as 20 minutes or up to an hour. Cut a Small Pad in half and warm the two halves between your hands for at least fifteen seconds. Lie down with your head on a pillow. Gently bend the pieces of the Small Pad so they touch all the skin directly below the eye. Relax your facial muscles and close your eyes. Gently place half a Small Pad with the flat side towards the eye, so that it is barely touching the lower eyelash. You may have to reshape the half Small Pad, as it is important that all areas touch the skin. Do not use tape or pressure to keep the pad in place. You may want to try this on only one eye first to be able to see the difference. Both eyes should then be done at the same time. It should be noted that this does not permanently remove bags under the eyes.

Arm and Wrist Discomfort

Small, Extended or Elongated Pad

The nerve running through the inside of the forearm and through the carpal tunnel gets trapped by swollen tissue (caused by repetitive motion/stress, scar tissue or fibrous ligaments), sometimes causing pain in the hand, fingers or even the forearm and elbow. This problem is common in people who use constant and repetitious hand and finger motions throughout the day. Using flexible tape or Ace bandage, secure one Small Pad over the center of the wrist on the inside where the nerve is trapped and another on the outside of the wrist. Or, for maximum effect, wrap a Extended or Elongated Pad completely around the wrist. It may take several days to experience a reduction in pain or it may take several weeks. The pads should continue to be worn for four to five weeks.

Top of Foot or Top of the Toes

Square, Medium, Small, Extended or Elongated Pad

Use flexible tape to tape the pad of choice to these areas and continue for two days after discomfort is gone.

Bottom of Foot

Square Pad

With flexible tape, fasten the Square Pad to the bottom of the foot at night or whenever you go to sleep. Your feet will feel great in the morning.

Because the bottom of the foot is richly endowed with blood vessels and nerve endings, the stronger magnetic field of the other magnets may cause discomfort. However, if the Square Pad is not effective, you may wish to try the stronger pads. Magnetic insoles, another magnetic application product, may be worn during the day or evening to increase circulation in the feet and legs. They may also alleviate or eliminate night-time leg cramps.

Hand Joints

Square or Medium Pad

The hand requires the use of two pads, one on top of, and one directly below the fingers. They are either taped on with flexible tape or placed inside a tight mitten so that the pads are very close to the skin. The best time for this use is at home at a time when it is possible to leave them on for long periods of time without removing them to wash the hands. Use of this procedure is recommended while sleeping for best results. In the hand, the discomfort may never disappear completely, so a continual program of at least one to two hours at night may have to be followed.

Hand Joints (cont.)

Magnetic *massage balls* may also be used to relieve discomfort in the hand joints. Take the *balls* out of their case and roll them in your hand. Or wear them inside a pair of gloves while you sleep. The magnetic field in the *balls* will increase circulation in the hands and help to relieve pain, including arthritis pain. Additionally, the *massage balls* can be used to stimulate the reflexology points in your hand, which helps to relieve tension and also to keep you alert. (To open the case, squeeze the ends, not the sides.)

Hips

Square, Medium or Large Pad

Tape either a Square Pad or Large Pad to the joint area in the hip first and then to any other area that you feel radiating discomfort. Always position the flexible tape in the ways that the stretch has the most benefit. Or wear the pad in your hip pocket. (Be sure to remove your wallet.) Continue use for one week after discomfort is gone.

A Large Pad may be used in place of the other pads. It covers a larger area and has Velcro strips on the back so you can place it inside clothing and it will stay in place. Care should be taken when going to the bathroom that you don't forget it is there and let it fall into the water. Since the Velcro can tear knitted underwear and pantyhose, you may wish to wear the Large Pad between your underwear and your outer clothing rather than next to the skin.

Small, Extended or Elongated Pad

To place the magnet properly on the knee, sit down, expose the knee and straighten your leg forward. As you do so you will see a depression on either side of your knee cap. You should use two pads, one in each depression in conjunction with a knee brace. An elastic knee brace is made by Ace and has side stabilizers. The knee brace is pulled up over the leg so half is above the knee and half below. The magnets are then placed under the brace in the two depressions. The pads and brace should be worn for at least a week, or even longer, after the discomfort is gone.

Menstrual Discomfort

Small, Extended or Elongated Pad

Place a magnet over each ovary just below the bikini line. Use flexible tape to hold them in place.

Neck

Square or Medium Pad

During the day, place the pad of choice over the center of the area on the neck and affix with flexible tape. At night for maximum benefit, a pad can be fastened to a cervical collar by attaching a piece of male Velcro to the gold surface. The collar is then placed around the neck in the usual manner. Remember that the pad must be close to the skin. It may be better for the pad to be first taped to the neck followed by the cervical collar. By not moving the neck at night, we allow the body, with the aid of the magnets, to do its job. Two days of use are recommended after the discomfort is gone.

The magnetic field strength of the Small, Extended and Elongated Pads may be too strong for use on the neck, but if the Square or Medium Pad is not effective, you may wish to try these stronger pads.

Phantom Limb Discomfort

Square, Small, Medium Extended or Elongated Pads

Phantom limb discomfort is caused by severed nerve endings continuing to send pain signals to the brain. Place a magnet right on the end of the stump and keep it there for at least thirty minutes after the cessation of pain.

Shoulder Discomfort

Small, Extended, Elongated, Square or Medium Pads

Often the discomfort in a shoulder radiates down from the side of the arm between the biceps and the triceps but the source of the pain is actually on your shoulder. In fact, the source is closer to your neck rather than the arm where the discomfort is prominent. To locate this area so you can best find the appropriate spot, take off your shirt and stand facing a mirror. Extend your hand straight up in the air over your head and you will see a valley between the round part of your shoulder and your neck. It is in this valley you should place the magnetic pad of choice. The pad should be secured with flexible tape (the Small, Elongated and Extended Pads should be secured with the long part going from front to back). If, after two days, there is still discomfort in the higher part of the arm or lower shoulder, place another pad on that area with flexible tape but always keep the first pad on the primary area. Use of the pads in these areas should continue for one week after the discomfort is gone. These areas are heavy muscle areas and require more care.

Square or Medium Pad

A Square or Medium Pad may be used to relieve a sinus discomfort by holding it up to your forehead or over the eyebrows or under the eyes for approximately 20 minutes or until the pain is gone. A headband may be used to hold the magnets in place.

The magnetic field strength of the Small, Extended and Elongated Pads in some instances may be too strong and cause discomfort, but if the Small or Medium Pad is not effective, you may wish to try these stronger pads.

Stress Discomfort

Small, Extended, or Elongated Pad

Stress discomfort is caused by tension in the shoulder muscles that go up the neck and are attached to the base of the skull. A flexible magnetic application pad may relieve the tension in the muscle, thereby relieving the discomfort. To find the best spot to relieve tension in the shoulder muscle, use your right hand to feel along the left shoulder muscle to find the motor point (aka: release point, trigger point), a hard pebble of muscle between the spine and the shoulder blade. Place a magnet over that motor point and over the motor point on the right side. Use flexible tape to hold the pad in place. A magnet can also be used right on the neck muscle at the base of the skull.

The extra strength of the Small, Extended and Elongated Pads may cause dizziness or other discomfort if used on the neck. For this reason you may wish to use a Small or Medium Pad, or place one of the other pads lower on the neck.

Jaw Discomfort

Square, Small, Medium, Extended or Elongated Pads

The nerve in the jaw can be the source of considerable discomfort for some people. Place one of the magnetic application pads over the joint to relieve discomfort. A headband may be used to hold the magnet in place. Since this pain is nerve related, it may be necessary to keep the magnet in place for an extended period of time to achieve results.

The magnetic field strength of a Small, Extennded or Elongated Pad may be too strong and cause discomfort, but if a Square or Medium Pad is not effective, you may wish to try these stronger pads.

Elbow & Shoulder Discomfort

Small, Extended or Elongated Pad

Although we say to locate the central point of maximum discomfort, that is not so easy in this situation. The discomfort from this form of tendonitis radiates down the forearm, but the actual source of the problem is the elbow. To determine the appropriate placement of a pad hold your arm straight in front of you and turn your hand so that the palm of your hand is facing out and your thumb is pointing down. You will now see a small depression above your elbow joint. That is the exact point—no higher or lower, even if the pain is in another area above or more often below. Using an Ace elbow bandage, pull the bandage over the arm until half is above the elbow and half is below. The right size bandage is important for comfort as well as circulation. Now take the pad of choice and slide it into the bandage over the small depression. To keep the pad from shifting in the bandage, you may want to attach a piece of male Velcro on top of the gold surface of the magnet. You can wear this all day and night, only taking it off to shower or bathe. How long it is used is different in every individual; however, it should be worn at least two days after all discomfort has disappeared.

Square or Medium Pad

Using flexible tape, place one of the pads half on the top of the hand and half on the bottom, covering the fleshy area at the base of the thumb which is part of the palm of the hand. You must tape it so that you have immobilized the thumb. The only way the thumb will get better is if it cannot be moved. This is in most cases a long process depending upon the age of the injury. Use the pad day and night, taking it off only to shower or bathe. Continue use for a week after discomfort is gone. Because we use the thumb for so many things, to insure that you do not reinjure the area, we add one week rather than two days.

Wrinkles on the Face

Square or Medium Pad

For large areas of wrinkles, use a Square or Medium Pad on each side of the face. Use this procedure at home so that the pads can be left in place overnight or for at least a few hours. It should be noted that this does not permanently remove wrinkles.

Wrist Strains

Square, Small, Medium, Elongated or Extended Pad

Slide the magnetic pad of choice into a wrist sweat band or Ace wrist elastic bandage. You will need the added stability of the wrist wrap to allow the pad to produce its maximum effect. To keep the pad from shifting use the same Velcro technique suggested for tennis elbow. Continue use at least two days after all discomfort has disappeared.

Magnetic Field Application for Total Body Wellness

In addition to using Magnetic Field Application to relieve local stress and discomfort, you can experience its benefits for your total body wellness by sleeping on a magnetic *mattress pad* and *pillow* and sitting on a magnetic *seat cushion*. They stimulate the circulatory and lymphatic systems, as well as balancing the energy flow, thus improving overall body functioning. According to Dr. Edward A. Hacmac, D.C., "when the body is placed within such a magnetic sleep system, kinesiology (muscle strength) testing shows each acupuncture meridian in the body is functioning in harmony within fifteen minutes. It logically follows that the longer a body remains in this environment, the more quickly it can balance itself."

Magnetic *mattresses*, *mattress pads*, and *pillows* are designed to provide a sound and restful sleep, so that one awakens with more energy and greater alertness. They reinforce the effect of the flexible magnetic application *pads*. For the bedridden they help to prevent bed sores. The magnets in these products have a strength of 800 gauss.

A magnetic *seat cushion* with attached back is especially valuable for persons who are unable to exercise or who sit for long periods during the day. Persons who work with computers often desire the benefit of the magnetic field provided by the *seat cushion*. The *seat* can be taken along on trips and used for sleeping as well as sitting, so that you have the benefit of Magnetic Field Application even when away from home. Remove wallet from hip pocket to prevent the demagnetizing of credit cards. The strength of the magnets in the *seat cushion* is 800 gauss.

Keeping yourself in a beneficial magnetic field during the day and all night long brings harmony and balance to your body, so that you feel better and function better, both physically and mentally.

Two other magnetic products contribute to total body wellness:

Magnetic *massage balls*, two 800-gauss magnetic *balls* in a case, can be used to give a relaxing massage to the entire body or to direct magnetic force to specific areas. The massage should be light but rapid. The faster the *balls* spin, the stronger the magnetic pulse and the deeper the penetration. When the *balls* are removed

from the case and rolled in the hand, the specially designed nodules on the surface stimulate the reflexology points on the hand, thus stimulating the corresponding organs of the body, relieving stress, and promoting mental alertness. You can also put the *balls* on the floor and roll your feet over them. To open the case, squeeze the ends, not the sides. When you replace the *balls* in the case, be sure the circle inscribed on each ball faces up. When the second *ball* is inserted, the first *ball* will revolve, so the circle on it faces down.

Magnetic *insoles*, with a strength of 350 gauss, increase energy flow and stimulate the circulation in the feet and legs, thus benefitting the whole body. They can be worn during all or part of the day and/ or during the evening. The massage nodules covering the *insoles* stimulate the reflexology points on the feet, thus stimulating the corresponding organs of the body, with a positive effect on overall well-being. Try both sides of the *insoles* to see which works better for you. The *insoles* may also alleviate or eliminate night-time leg cramps.

ISF

Section 3

Magnetic Field
Application

Articles and Excerpts
Concerning Magnetic
Field Application

In order to avoid unnecessary injury to your horse and to obtain the maximum benefit from the unique features of magnet therapy the following suggestions and recommendations are offered:

1. Consult with your vet to determine whether magnet therapy is an appropriate therapy for the specific injury.

2. Do not place a [magnetic pad] on an area that has had paint or liniment on it. The petrochemical base of many preparations will tend to degrade the polyethylene matrix of the pads. Wash all areas of application very thoroughly with soap and water and leave uncovered for approximately 24 hours prior to the application of the magnetic pads.

3. The pads should be placed as close to the skin as possible without causing excessive pressure to, or aggravation of, the condition being treated. It is also recommended the area be checked to make sure it is thoroughly dry and has remained clean.

4. Placement:

Leg. The large pad ("Flex") should be placed on the back of the canon with the wider end down and with the soft cotton side facing the leg. Wrap the leg as usual with regular leg wrapping bandages to secure the pad (the hook style material on the back of the pad will serve to anchor the pad within the bandage).

For use on the front of the canon, place the pad on the shin with the wide end up and cotton side also facing the leg, and affix in a similar manner as the back.

NOTE: Another, stronger, type of application using several strip- or band-type pads can be substituted for any of the applications mentioned here and is simplified through the use of a soft cotton cloth cover specifically designed for the purpose. This cover makes it possible to target 1, 2 or 3 separate magnets to specific areas and also select identical types (strip, band, mini or card) or intermix them depending upon the desired effect.

Forte Circle. Use a magnetic pad of the appropriate size and shape. Place a small piece of hook-style material on the surface opposite the soft cotton side to help keep the pad from shifting inside the wrapping (see "Note" above for possible alternative). For some very difficult to bandage areas, tape will most likely be the best and only alternative. Should this prove to be the case, we advise *against* using a tape with limited flexibility or strong adhesive qualities as it may cause damage to the magnet or your patient.

Pastern and Splint. The pads are placed on the intended area and wrapped as advised in the previous applications.

5. Once applied, a pad should remain in place for at least 4-6 hours, increasing by two hour intervals to a maximum length of application of approximately 20 hours per day. This gradual increase provides an opportunity for accurate assessment of the effect the application is having upon the condition being treated. If the area begins to swell it could be a sign that the modality was begun too early and should be discontinued. The area should be completely cooled down and

reevaluated before beginning again after the swelling has begun to recede.

6. A recommended modality for use of the leg pads is to apply them in the morning during the normal routine, remove before the evening feed, then reapply when the legs are done up for the evening. The pads remain in place until morning, when they are removed again for a short time before starting the routine again. This routine will allow two opportunities per day for examination of the effectiveness of the therapy, and will also allow you to observe any signs of, and take corrective action for, pressure or friction sensitivity.

7. When applying any pads be careful not to place them too close to joints as the continuous flexing and torquing in this area will

eventually cause a breakdown in the material the pad is made from. Cracking, however, will not decrease the effectiveness of the pad—the pads may even be cut in half without decreasing their strength or effectiveness, and can only be destroyed by extreme heat (melting), degaussing (requires an industrial-strength electromagnet) or chemical contamination as mentioned earlier. Should your pad suffer damage in the form of cracking, simply use a strong strapping tape (duct tape is a good choice) on the back to restore its integrity. It is well to keep this adaptability of the pads in mind should you run into any special or difficult treatment requirements.

8. The degree of severity of the injury is the determining factor as to length of treatment. Naturally, a severe tendonitis will take longer to heal than a slight sprain. Please work with your vet to determine the appropriate treatment time. Most injuries will begin to exhibit signs of dramatic change within a few days.

9. After the injury has healed, it is recommended that a regular routine of application be maintained as a preventive measure. By increasing the circulation to areas being placed, or about to be placed under stress, the chances for an injury occurring are greatly reduced. IMPORTANT: It should be remembered that certain injuries to the foreleg are sometimes incorrectly assumed to be healed when the lameness has subsided. This is a very dangerous assumption as it has been found in many cases that signs of lameness do not correlate well with the extent of the injury. Caution should be exercised against returning a horse to its normal routine prematurely when it has suffered this type of injury.

10. The pads should not be used while exercising or bathing the horse. If the pads were left on during a workout, the horse could suffer further injury due to the tremendous buildup of heat in the area. While water will not damage the magnetic material itself, the cotton facing will deteriorate more rapidly under these conditions. When the cotton face becomes worn or soiled to the point that it cannot be restored by washing in a mild soap and water solution, simply peel it off and replace it with a similar material (adhesive-backed moleskin found in the Dr. Scholl's human foot care section

of your local drug store or grocery makes a great substitute).

Cautions:

Do Not Apply Magnetic Type Pads...

. . . If the horse has an active untreated infection
. . . To an area with an acute injury—cool thoroughly
. . . To a hematoma less than three days old
. . . On or near open wounds
. . . When you would normally use ice
. . . While exercising or bathing the horse
. . . Without consulting your veterinarian

Also of interest for the horse owner in the area of useful magnetic products, it has been found that the *seat cushion* or the *horse blanket* is highly appreciated when placed on the back after a long day under a saddle.

You may discover many other worthwhile applications and uses for these amazing new products and devices yourself—like the discovery that your cat or dog has developed a very strong attraction for sleeping on your bed since you got the new magnetic mattress.

References

Bansal, Dr. H.L., *Magnet Therapy*

Bansal, Dr. H.L., and Bansal, Dr. R.S., *Magnetic Cure for Common Diseases*

Becker, Robert O., MD, *Cross Currents*

Becker, Robert O., MD, & Selden, Gary, *The Body Electric*

Breakthrough Media, Inc., *Magnetic Devices for Self Use*

Brennan, Barbara Ann, *Hands of Light*

Brennan, Barbara Ann, *Light Emerging*

Callahan, Phillip S., *Ancient Mysteries, Modern Visions*

Cerney, J. V., *Acupuncture Without Needles*

Davis, Albert Roy, & Rawls, Walter C., Jr., *Magnetism and Its Effects on The Living System*

Davis, Albert Roy, & Rawls, Walter C., Jr., *The Magnetic Effect*

Davis, Albert Roy, & Rawls, Walter C., Jr., *The Rainbow In Your Hands*

Hacmac, Edward A., DC, *An Overview of Biomagnetic Therapeutics*

Hannemann, Holger, *Magnet Therapy: Balancing Your Body's Energy Flow for Self-Healing*, Sterling Publishing Company, 387 Park Avenue South, New York, NY, 10016

Lee, Carroll, *The Kryon Writings*, Books I, II, III. 1155 Camino Del Mar #422, Del Mar, CA 92014

Kervran, C. L., *Biological Transmutation*

O'Brien, Jim, Revolutionary New Magnetic Therapy KO's Arthritis Pain, *Your Health*, April 6, 1993

Payne, Dr. Buryl, *The Body Magnetic*

Payne, Dr. Buryl, *Getting Started in Magnetic Healing*

Suplee, Curt, Magnetism—The Force That's Always With You, *The Washington Post*, Page H1, December 14, 1994